Bunny Days

Celebrating Easter with Rhymes, Songs, Projects, Games, and Snacks

By SUSAN OLSON HIGGINS

Illustrated by MARION HOPPING EKBERG

Totline® Publications

A Division of Frank Schaffer Publications, Inc.

Torrance, California

Thank you to my incredible sons, friends, relatives, and those who have given their support and shared the love and joyful spirit of this holiday throughout the years. God bless you!

And, thank you to those who shared an idea or assisted in putting this collection together, especially, Linda Marooney, Mary Burns, Ruth Begalke, Barbara Lapp, Rev. and Mrs. Benjamin Pent, and, in memory of, V.I. Wexner, editor of the original book.

—Susan Olson Higgins

Managing Editor: Mina McMullin

Editor: Elizabeth McKinnon

Contributing Editors: Kathleen Cubley, Susan Hodges, Jean Warren

Copyeditor: Kathy Zaun

Editorial Assistant: Mary Newmaster

Graphic Designer (Interior): Jill Kaufman

Graphic Designer (Cover): Brenda Mann Harrison

Production Manager: Janie Schmidt

Portions of this text are taken from *The Bunny Book* by Susan Olson Higgins, originally published by Pumpkin Press Publishing House.

ISBN: 1-57029-271-X

Printed in the United States of America
Published by Totline® Publications
23740 Hawthorne Blvd.
Torrance, CA 90505

Contents

Celebrating Easter

As spring bursts into bloom, it brings new life to the earth along with one of the most important holidays of the year, Easter. For children, the season is heralded by familiar symbols—spring flowers, baby animals, decorated baskets, and, of course, eggs and bunnies.

Colored Eggs Everywhere

Eggs—which represent new life—have been colored and exchanged for hundreds of years. Ancient Egyptians dyed eggs and gave them as gifts. In England, friends wrote messages to one another on colored eggs. And today, in many parts of the world, the practice of coloring and exchanging eggs continues as a happy springtime custom.

The Easter Bunny

In the United States and elsewhere, children wait for the Easter Bunny to bring and hide colored eggs for them to find on Easter morning. How did this tradition begin? Here is one popular tale:

Long ago in Germany, there lived an old, loving woman who adored children. Each year, she would give the children gifts to celebrate spring. One year, she had nothing to give because she had grown very poor. All she had were some eggs. She did not want to disappoint the children, so she colored the eggs and hid them in the grass. When the children came, the old woman sent them outside to search for their gifts. Just as they uncovered the eggs, they saw a big rabbit hopping away. "That rabbit must have left the eggs for us!" the children cried. And from that time on, children everywhere have looked forward to hunting for the colored eggs left by the Easter Bunny.

Bunny Tracks

For a fun surprise on Easter morning, make some bunny tracks for your child to discover. Just dip two fingers into flour or baking soda and press them onto a dark-colored surface to make a line of bunny "footprints" leading to a hidden egg or two.

Easter Basket Treats

If you would like to cut down on the amount of candy in your child's Easter basket, here are a few suggestions for other kinds of treats you might include:

* stickers

* sidewalk chalk

* plastic eggs

* crayons

* bubble solution

Rhymes & Songs

Springtime Morning

The sun is up,
   (Raise arms high.)

The sun is up,
   (Keep arms up.)

On a springtime morning!

Open the door,
   (Pretend to open door.)

Step outside.
   (Take a step.)

Let's go exploring!
   (Cup hand above eye.)

As you and your child "go exploring," talk about the springtime things you see around you.

Susan Olson Higgins

A Ring of Flowers

Sung to: "Ring Around the Rosie"

A ring of springtime flowers
   (Sit on floor in a circle.)

Made from April showers.

Tulips, buttercups—

They all pop up!
   (Jump to feet.)

Susan Olson Higgins

Bouncing Into Spring

See the little lamb,
Bouncing in the field.

See the fluffy bunny,
Bouncing with such zeal.

See the little duckling,
Bouncing here and there.

See the newborn colt,
Bouncing everywhere.

See the little yellow chick,
Bouncing round the hen.

See me bouncing in the field,
Then bouncing home again!

Encourage your child to act out the bouncing
movements as you recite the rhyme.

Susan Olson Higgins

Easter Riddles

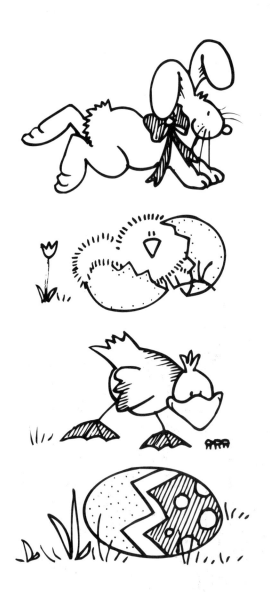

I hop and I jump.
My ears are big and funny.
My tail is puffy.
I am the Easter (Bunny).

Where corn is about,
I pick, peck, pick.
I come from an egg.
I am an Easter (chick.)

I waddle and quack,
And with any luck,
I will catch a fat bug.
I am an Easter (duck).

I am oval in shape.
I can roll by your leg.
I am colored, then hidden.
I am an Easter (egg).

Each time you recite a verse, pause
at the end of the last line and let
your child name the rhyming word.

Susan Olson Higgins

You Can Be a Bunny

Sniff, sniff, sniff.
(Sniff three times.)

Hop, hop, hop.
(Hop three times.)

Shake your little bunny tail,
(Shake backside.)

Then stop, stop, stop.
(Stand quietly.)

Twitch, twitch, twitch.
(Twitch nose three times.)

Hop out of sight.
(Stoop down low.)

Crawl into your bunny burrow
(Pretend to snuggle into burrow.)

For the night.
(Pretend to sleep.)

Susan Olson Higgins

A Bunny Fingerplay

Five little bunnies
  (Hold up five fingers.)

Hopped up a hill.

One stopped to pick

A yellow daffodil.

Four little bunnies
  (Hold up four fingers.)

Hopped past me.

One stopped to nibble

By the old willow tree.

Three little bunnies
  (Hold up three fingers.)

Hopped near a brook.

One heard a splash

And stopped to take a look.

Two little bunnies
  (Hold up two fingers.)

Hopped past a mouse.

One stopped to visit

In its teeny-tiny house.

One little bunny
  (Hold up one finger.)

Hopped down the knoll.

Then he disappeared

In his rabbit hole.
  (Hop finger behind back.)

Susan Olson Higgins

Silly Little Bunny

Silly little bunny,

Wrinkle your nose.
  (Wrinkle nose.)

Bend down low
  (Stoop down.)

And touch your toes.
  (Touch toes.)

Now, little bunny,

Stand up tall.
  (Stand tall.)

Wiggle your ears—

Don't let them fall.
  (Wiggle hands above head.)

Happy little bunny,

Spin around.
  (Spin.)

Show where your cotton tail

Can be found.
  (Wiggle backside.)

Hurry, little bunny,

Jump up high.
  (Jump.)

Hop away before

Easter passes by!
  (Hop away.)

Susan Olson Higgins

Off to Bed, Now

The Easter Bunny never arrives
Until you're in bed and you close your eyes.

He never visits a child who's awake,
So go right to sleep—for your own sake.

If you go right to sleep, he will hide some treats.
He will fill your basket with eggs and sweets.

He always knows if you've gone to bed,
So hop right in and cover your head.

While you are sleeping, that's when Bunny brings
All those delicious Eastery things!

Susan Olson Higgins

It's Time to Hide Your Eggs

Sung to: "Frère Jacques"

Are you sleeping, are you sleeping,
  (Lie down on floor.)

Easter Bunny, Easter Bunny?

It's time to hide your eggs now,
  (Stand up.)

It's time to hide your eggs now.

Hop away, hop away.
  (Hop around room.)

Susan Olson Higgins

Hoppy Bunny

Hop, hop, hop to the left.
  (Hop left.)

Hop, hop, hop to the right.
  (Hop right.)

Easter Bunny, hide your eggs,
  (Pretend to hide eggs.)

Then hop, hop out of sight.
  (Hop away.)

Susan Olson Higgins

Oh, Easter Bunny, Hurry!

Sung to: "Yankee Doodle"

Little bunny bounding off,

His cotton tail flip-flopping.

He is in an Easter rush,

He has no time for stopping.

Hopping, bobbing as he goes,

Little bunny, scurry.

Hide the eggs for boys and girls.

Oh, Easter Bunny, hurry!

Let your child pretend to be the Easter
Bunny as you sing the song.

Susan Olson Higgins

The Easter Bunny's Here

Sung to: "The Farmer in the Dell"

The Easter Bunny's here,
The Easter Bunny's here.
Heigh-ho! It's Easter day.
The Easter Bunny's here.

The Bunny hides his eggs,
The Bunny hides his eggs.
Heigh-ho! It's Easter day.
The Bunny hides his eggs.

The children all wake up,
The children all wake up.
Heigh-ho! It's Easter day.
The children all wake up.

The children hunt for eggs,
The children hunt for eggs.
Heigh-ho! It's Easter day.
The children hunt for eggs.

They fill their baskets full,
They fill their baskets full.
Heigh-ho! It's Easter day.
They fill their baskets full.

Additional verses: The children count the eggs; The families gather round; The families go to church; The Easter Bunny rests.

Susan Olson Higgins

My Easter Basket

Sung to: "A-Tisket, A-Tasket"

A-tisket, a-tasket,

I have an Easter basket.

Come and put an egg inside

My pretty Easter basket.

Hide plastic eggs or paper egg shapes. As you sing the song with your child, let him hunt for the eggs and put them into an Easter basket.

Susan Olson Higgins

Searching for Eggs

Searching high,

Searching low.

There are eggs

Everywhere I go!

Susan Olson Higgins

Just for Fun

Blossoming Branch

You Will Need

scissors
white tissue paper
ruler
pencil
brown crayon
light blue construction paper
bowl
glue

1. Cut white tissue paper into 2-inch squares.

2. Help your child twist each square around the eraser end of a pencil to make "blossoms."

3. Using a brown crayon, draw a bare branch on a piece of light blue construction paper.

4. Give the paper to your child and set out a small bowl of glue.

5. Invite your child to dip the tissue blossoms into the glue and place them on and around the branch on his paper.

Easter Chick

You Will Need

scissors
cardboard egg carton
crayons or markers
cotton balls
washable yellow marker
glue
black and orange construction paper

1. Cut an egg cup out of a cardboard egg carton and trim the edges.

2. Ask your child to decorate the cup with crayons or markers.

3. Lightly stroke two cotton balls with a washable yellow marker to add a pale yellow tint.

4. Help your child glue one of the cotton balls inside the egg cup and the other ball on top of the first one to create a chick body.

5. Give her eye shapes cut from black construction paper and a beak shape cut from orange construction paper to glue onto the top ball to complete her Easter Chick.

Sandy Duckling

You Will Need

scissors
white construction paper
yellow tempera paint
sand
paintbrush

1. Cut a duck shape, as shown in the illustration, out of white construction paper.

2. Mix yellow tempera paint with a small amount of sand.

3. Let your child paint the duck shape with the sandy paint to create a textured effect.

4. When the paint has dried, help him display his Sandy Duckling as an Easter decoration.

   Another Idea: You may wish to glue a few small, yellow, fluffy feathers to the duck's tail after the glue has dried.

Bunny Ears

You Will Need

- scissors
- ruler
- white construction paper
- stapler
- pink crayon or marker
- tape

1. Cut two 2-by-12-inch strips from a piece of white construction paper.

2. Staple the ends of the strips together to make a headband, adjusting it to fit around your child's head.

3. Cut two bunny ear shapes from white construction paper.

4. Invite your child to color the inner parts of the ears pink.

5. Staple the ears to the headband and cover the staples with tape. Help your child put on her headband.

6. If she wishes, let her wear her Bunny Ears while acting out the movements of "You Can Be a Bunny," page 11.

   Another Idea: To complete the bunny look, dab pink lipstick onto your child's nose. Also help her tape on a cotton ball "tail."

Fuzzy Bunny

You Will Need

white construction paper
scissors
bowl
glue
cotton balls
paintbrush

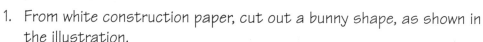

1. From white construction paper, cut out a bunny shape, as shown in the illustration.

2. Give your child a small bowl of glue and some fluffed-out cotton balls.

3. Invite him to brush the glue onto the bunny shape and place the fluffy cotton on top of the glue.

4. When the bunny is completely covered, help your child glue on one round cotton ball for a tail.

5. Display his Fuzzy Bunny as an Easter decoration, if he wishes.

Potato Bunny

You Will Need

knife
potato
toothpicks
raisins
scissors
construction paper
cotton ball

1. Cut one end off a large potato, stand the potato upright, and let your child help you turn it into a bunny.

2. Break toothpicks in half and use them to attach raisin eyes and a raisin nose to one side of the potato.

3. Break two more toothpicks in half and stick the pieces into the potato on either side of the bunny nose for whiskers.

4. Cut bunny ears out of construction paper and attach them to the top of the potato with toothpicks.

5. Use another toothpick to attach a cotton ball for a bunny tail.

6. Let your child hold the Potato Bunny while telling bunny stories or singing bunny songs.

Easter Bookmark

You Will Need

scissors
ruler
white construction paper
washable ink pads
green marker
pen
hole punch and yarn or ribbon (optional)

1. Cut a 2-by-7-inch strip out of white construction paper to use for making a bookmark.

2. Set out one or two colors of washable ink pads.

3. Invite your child to decorate the bookmark with colored fingerprint "eggs."

4. Let him add a few green marker designs to represent Easter grass.

5. On the back of the bookmark, print "Happy Easter," and help your child sign his name.

6. If you wish, use a hole punch to make a hole in one end of the bookmark and tie on a colorful piece of yarn or ribbon.

7. Encourage your child to give his bookmark as an Easter gift.

Easter Hat

You Will Need

ruler	diluted glue
thin, 9-inch paper plate	paintbrush
gift-wrap	stapler
scissors	tape
bowl	yarn

1. Find a thin, 9-inch paper plate to use for making a hat.

2. Let your child help choose gift-wrap in a pattern she would like to use for decorating.

3. Cut a 9-inch circle out of the gift-wrap and set out a small bowl of diluted glue.

4. Let your child brush glue all over the back of the paper plate and help her place the gift-wrap circle on top of the glue. Allow the plate to dry.

5. Cut a slit from the edge of the plate to the center, overlap the edges, and staple them together to form a cone-shaped hat.

6. Tape pieces of yarn to the sides of the hat for ties.

   Another Idea: Instead of using gift-wrap, let your child decorate her hat with collage materials, such as colorful paper and fabric scraps, yarn, lace, ribbon, or sequins.

Potato-Print Eggs

You Will Need

scissors
white construction paper
knife
small, oval potato
paper towels
two shallow containers
two colors of tempera paint

1. Make a "plate" by cutting a piece of white construction paper into a large circle.

2. Cut a small potato in half lengthwise. Carefully "carve" a simple design on the flat edge of the potato.

3. For paint pads, place folded paper towels in two shallow containers. Pour one color of tempera paint into one container and another color of paint into the second container.

4. Invite your child to press the cut sides of the potato halves onto the paint pads, then onto the paper circle to create a plateful of colored "eggs."

Eggs in a Basket

You Will Need

    brown paper grocery bag
    scissors
    gift-wrap
    construction paper
    glue

1. From a brown paper grocery bag, cut out a large basket shape, as shown in the illustration.

2. Cut egg shapes out of colorful gift-wrap and/or construction paper.

3. Give your child the basket shape and invite her to glue the colored eggs on it any way she wishes.

4. Display her egg-filled basket as an Easter decoration.

Chalk Eggs

You Will Need

scissors
white or pastel-colored construction paper
colored chalk
cup
water

1. Cut large egg shapes out of white or pastel-colored construction paper.

2. Set out colored chalk and a small cup of water.

3. Let your child decorate the egg shapes with designs that won't smear by dipping the chalk pieces into the water and using them to draw on the eggs.

4. When the eggs are dry, use them to create an Easter display on a wall or a door, if you wish.

Woven Easter Basket

You Will Need

- plastic berry basket
- yarn or ribbon pieces
- Easter grass
- chenille stem
- paper egg cutouts and crayons or markers (optional)

1. Set out a plastic berry basket along with colorful ribbon or yarn pieces.

2. Tie one end of a piece of ribbon or yarn to a corner of the basket.

3. Give the basket to your child and show her how to begin weaving the other end of the ribbon in and out of the basket holes.

4. Encourage her to continue weaving any way she wishes, helping her to tie on more ribbon pieces as needed.

5. When she has finished, help her fill her basket with Easter grass and attach a chenille stem for a handle.

6. Give her paper egg cutouts to decorate with crayons or markers to add to her basket, if she wishes.

Tissue Paper Eggs

You Will Need

hard-cooked eggs
colored tissue paper
paintbrush
glue
egg carton

1. Set out cooled, hard-cooked eggs.

2. Invite your child to tear colored tissue paper into small pieces.

3. Let him brush glue on one area of an egg at a time and then cover the glue with pieces of tissue, overlapping the pieces as he works.

4. When the egg is completely covered with tissue, help him brush on a final coat of glue and place the egg in an empty egg carton to dry.

5. Encourage him to decorate as many eggs as he wishes.

Crayon-Resist Eggs

You Will Need

Easter egg dyes
white crayon
hard-cooked eggs
glass or plastic container

1. Prepare Easter egg dyes as directed on the package.

2. Invite your child to use a white crayon to draw designs on cooled, hard-cooked eggs.

3. Help her dip the eggs into the egg dyes, watching together as her crayon designs "magically" appear.

4. Place her dyed eggs in a clean glass or plastic container to dry.

    Another Idea: Let your child experiment using other colors of crayons to draw designs on eggs before dyeing them.

Natural Egg Dyes

You Will Need

uncooked white eggs
saucepan
measuring cup
water
onion skins, tea leaves, or blackberries

1. Place uncooked white eggs in a saucepan with two cups of water.

2. Let your child help you experiment with adding onion skins, tea leaves, or blackberries to the water. (Onion skins will dye the eggs yellow; tea leaves will dye them brown; and blackberries will dye them blue.)

3. Bring the water to a boil, then simmer for at least 7 minutes.

4. Allow the eggs to remain in the colored water, turning them often, until they reach the desired shade.

   Another Idea: Experiment with making dyes from other natural items, such as spinach leaves, beets, or grape juice.

   Hint: Use eggs colored with natural dyes for decorating rather than eating.

Colorful Eggshell Collage

You Will Need

shells from colored Easter eggs
bowls
construction paper
glue
cotton swab

1. Save the shells from colored Easter eggs. Lightly crush them, then put the pieces into a bowl.

2. Set out a piece of construction paper and a small bowl of glue.

3. Let your child use a cotton swab to glue the eggshell pieces on her paper any way she wishes to create a Colorful Eggshell Collage.

Musical Blossoms

You Will Need

- three or more players
- scissors
- colored paper
- masking tape
- music

1. For each player, cut a large flower shape out of colored paper, such as butcher paper or gift-wrap.

2. With masking tape, lightly attach the flower shapes to the floor in a large circle.

3. Invite each player to sit on a "blossom."

4. Start some music, and have the players begin walking around the circle. As they do so, remove one of the blossoms.

5. When you stop the music, have the players scurry to find a blossom to sit on or to share by touching it with a finger, a toe, an elbow, or in some other way.

6. Continue starting and stopping the music, each time removing a blossom and having the players share fewer and fewer blossoms.

7. End the game when all the players are in a pile, giggling as they share the last blossom.

Colored Egg Hunt

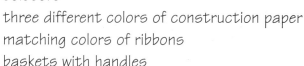

You Will Need

one or more players

scissors

three different colors of construction paper

matching colors of ribbons

baskets with handles

1. Cut six to ten egg shapes from each of three different colors of construction paper, such as pink, yellow, and blue.

2. Tie a pink ribbon to one basket handle, a yellow ribbon to a second basket handle, and a blue ribbon to a third basket handle.

3. Hide the egg shapes around the room where your child can easily reach them.

4. Give her one of the baskets and invite her to search for the eggs that match the color of the ribbon tied to it.

5. When she has found all the eggs of one color, have her hunt for the other colors of eggs until they have all been discovered and placed in their appropriate baskets.

Give Bunny a Tail

You Will Need

three or more players
scissors
white paper
masking tape
cotton balls

1. Cut a large bunny shape from white paper and attach it to a wall with masking tape.

2. Make a "bunny tail" for each player by attaching a loop of masking tape, rolled sticky side out, to a cotton ball.

3. Have the players take turns closing their eyes and sticking their cotton bunny tails on the bunny shape.

4. Let the player whose tail came closest to being in the right spot have the first turn for the next round of the game.

Bunnies, Find Your Burrows

You Will Need

three or more players
scissors
construction paper or gift-wrap

1. For each player, cut two matching egg shapes from a different color of construction paper or gift-wrap.

2. Hide one egg from each pair somewhere in the room and hand out the remaining eggs to the "bunny" players.

3. Have the bunnies hop around the room and search for their "burrows," which contain their matching eggs.

4. Whenever a bunny finds its burrow, ask it to stay there until all the matching eggs have been found.

5. At the end of the game, let the bunny who first found its burrow help hide the eggs for the next round.

Jellybean Guess

You Will Need

two or more players
jellybeans
jar with lid

1. Put a handful of jellybeans into a jar with a lid.

2. Give the jar to each player and ask him or her to guess how many jellybeans are inside it.

3. Take a turn, making a guess yourself.

4. Together, open the jar and count the jellybeans.

5. Let the player whose guess was closest choose a jellybean "prize."

6. Continue playing the game as long as you wish.

Egg Obstacle Course

You Will Need

- one or more players
- obstacles
- yarn or string
- hard-cooked or plastic egg
- small prize

1. On the floor, set out several "obstacles," such as pillows, chairs, furniture cushions, or boxes.

2. Make a yarn or string pathway around the obstacles.

3. Place a hard-cooked or plastic egg at the beginning of the pathway and a small prize, such as an Easter sticker or cutout, at the end.

4. Invite your child to try rolling the egg along the pathway until she reaches the other end and claims her prize.

Bunny's Favorite Carrot Sticks

carrots

plain yogurt

powdered salad dressing mix

1. Let your child help you wash and peel several carrots.

2. Cut the carrots into sticks.

3. Spoon plain yogurt into a small bowl, add powdered salad dressing, mix to taste, and let your child stir the mixture until it is well blended.

4. Serve the yogurt mixture as a dip for the Bunny's Favorite Carrot Sticks.

   Hint: Younger children can "peel" the carrots by scraping them with the bowl of a metal spoon.

Bunnied Eggs

hard-cooked eggs
mayonnaise
paprika (optional)
raisins

1. Slice each hard-cooked egg in half lengthwise.

2. Place the yolk in a small bowl and let your child use a fork to mash it and mix it with a little mayonnaise.

3. Spoon the yolk mixture back into the egg halves, and sprinkle on a little paprika, if desired.

4. Make a bunny on top of one of the egg yolk mixtures, using one raisin for a head and two raisins for ears.

5. Give your child three more raisins and invite her to make a bunny on the other egg half.

6. Serve the Bunnied Eggs as a snack or at lunchtime.

Bunny Cheese Sandwich

slice of bread
grated cheese
olive half

1. Use a cookie cutter to cut a bunny shape out of a slice of bread.

2. Let your child sprinkle grated cheese on the bread bunny and add an olive half for a tail.

3. Place the sandwich under the broiler for a few minutes until the cheese is bubbly.

4. Allow the Bunny Cheese Sandwich to cool before serving.

Egg-in-a-Basket

slice of bread
butter
egg

1. Use a round cookie cutter or the rim of a drinking glass to cut a circle out of the center of a slice of bread.

2. Butter both sides of the bread, including the cut-out circle.

3. In a frying pan, lightly brown the bread and the bread circle on both sides, adding more butter as needed.

4. Crack open an egg, drop it into the hole in the bread slice, and fry it with the bread until it is done to taste, turning it once, if you wish.

5. Serve the Egg-in-a-Basket, with the toasted bread circle on the side.

Easter Cookies

sugar cookie dough
prepared frosting
tubes of icing
cookie sprinkles

1. Make or purchase sugar cookie dough.

2. Roll out the dough and let your child use a cookie cutter to cut it into egg shapes.

3. Bake the cookies according to the recipe or package directions.

4. Set out plastic knives, prepared frosting, tubes of icing, and cookie sprinkles.

5. Invite your child to help you turn the cookies into "Easter eggs" by decorating them any way he wishes.

Easter Snack Basket

pipe cleaner
small, paper bathroom cup
salad sprouts or lettuce
seedless grapes

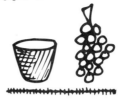

1. Make a paper cup basket by attaching a pipe cleaner handle to a small, paper bathroom cup.

2. Invite your child to put salad sprouts or shredded lettuce into the basket for Easter grass.

3. Let her complete her Easter Snack Basket by adding seedless grape "eggs."

Another Idea: Instead of using grapes, let your child fill her basket with raisins, nuts, dried fruit bits, or fresh fruit pieces.